📖 Need to Read SERIES

Make My Day

ROBERT C. SAVAGE

Tyndale House Publishers, Inc.
WHEATON, ILLINOIS

Front cover illustration by Robert C. Hayes

Adapted for the Need to Read Series from *Pocket Smiles* copyright © 1984 and *Pocket Wisdom* copyright © 1984 by Robert C. Savage.

ISBN 0-8423-3896-9
Library of Congress Catalog Card Number 90-71455
Copyright © 1990 by Robert C. Savage.
All rights reserved
Printed in the United States of America

95 94 93 92 91
9   8   7   6   5   4   3   2   1

CONTENTS

CHAPTER 1 *People Are Funny* ... PAGE *1*
(Human Nature)

CHAPTER 2 *Watch Out!* ... PAGE *9*
(Warnings)

CHAPTER 3 *Just for Fun* ... PAGE *13*
(Jokes)

CHAPTER 4 *Time to Work* ... PAGE *35*
(Job Related)

CHAPTER 5 *Good Thinking* ... PAGE *43*
(Wisdom)

CHAPTER 6 *Looking Up* ... PAGE *49*
(Motivational)

CHAPTER 7 *Down Home* ... PAGE *55*
(Home and Family)

CHAPTER 8 *Time for God* ... PAGE *61*
(Faith)

Word List ... PAGE *69*

CHAPTER 1
People Are Funny

People are funny! We all want to live long lives, but no one wants to get old!

The one who rows the boat will not have time to rock it.

What people do we like the best? The ones who don't keep telling us what we do wrong.

Tell a man there are 300 billion stars in the sky. He'll believe you. Tell the same man a park bench has just been painted. He will have to touch it to be sure.

We fight for the right to say what we think. So why do we say so much without thinking?

A hearty laugh and a sunny smile make the best cure around.

The less a man knows, the more he thinks he knows it all.

To make a mistake is common and normal.
To admit a mistake is very rare.

Aren't people funny? They spend money they don't have. They buy things they don't need. All to impress people they don't like.

It is too bad people can't swap problems with each other. For they all claim to know how to solve the other person's problem.

No one has given me as much trouble as myself. (Dwight L. Moody)

A little boy was playing with his blocks. "I am building a church," he told his father. "We have to be very quiet."
    The father had always taught his son to behave well in church. Now it seemed the boy was catching on. "And why do we have to be quiet?" the father asked.
    "Shhhh," the boy whispered. "Because the people are asleep."

Why are women's minds cleaner than men's? They change them more often.

Congress is so strange. A man gets up and says nothing. No one listens. Then they all argue about it.

Men wear their hair in three ways: parted, unparted, and departed.

Where does the man who owns his own home spend his time? In the hardware store.

Isn't this crazy? These days, when someone pays in cash, you wonder if his credit is good.

Want to get rid of a friend who pesters you all the time? Lend him some money. You'll never see him again.

An old man had a party for his one hundredth birthday. He was asked if he had any comments to make. "Well," he said. "I didn't know I was going to live this long. If I did, I'd have taken better care of myself."

I love mankind. It's people I can't stand.

A man stopped for dinner at a seafood place. He was in a hurry. He said roughly to the waitress,

"Do you serve crabs?"

"We serve anyone," she said. "What would you like?"

A grouchy man went to a diner for breakfast. "Bring me two eggs," he barked. "Boil one and scramble the other."

Soon the waitress returned with his food. "Take it back," he ordered. "You scrambled the wrong one!"

Al: Sue, will you marry me?
Sue: No, but I will always admire your good taste.

Some people cause joy *wherever* they go. Other people cause joy *whenever* they go.

I never care about something until I find out it's none of my business.

An old friend dropped by to pay a visit. She talked and talked and talked. At last she left. The little girl in the house said, "I'm glad she's gone. She was so boring!"

"But, dear," the mother said, "she only stayed an hour."

"I know," the girl replied. "But she stays longer in an hour than most people do in a whole week."

I can keep a secret. It's just the people I tell it to. They're the ones who blab it to others.

Four women got into an awful fight. After a lot of yelling, one of them said, "I'm going to the sheriff."

The other three all wanted to get there first. They all rushed to the sheriff's office. They barged in and began to blame each other.

The sheriff didn't know what to do. All four were talking at once. At last he came up with a wise answer. "All right," he said, "I'll hear you one at a time. The oldest one can speak first."

That closed the case.

Joe: Moe, you shouldn't worry so much. It doesn't do a bit of good.
Moe: Sure it does! Ninety percent of the things I worry about never happen.

CHAPTER 2
Watch Out!

The only things some people care about are none of their business.

Don't stretch the truth. It may very well snap back.

One of life's *hardest* jobs is to keep up the *"easy"* payments.

Bad habits are like a good bed. They are easy to get into but hard to get out of.

The yoke of the Lord Jesus will never fit a stiff neck.

Unless Jesus Christ is Lord *of* all, he cannot be Lord *at* all.

If you are *unkind,* you are the *wrong kind!*

Vacant lots and vacant minds are alike. They become dumping grounds for a lot of rubbish.

Nothing is more often "opened by mistake" than the mouth.

Are you helping with the problem? Or are you a part of the problem?

CHAPTER 3
Just for Fun

Some people battle to the top. Others bottle to the bottom.

The trouble with letting off steam is that it gets you into more hot water.

Don't give someone a piece of your mind. You need it all yourself!

A lot of people have trouble with their cars. The engine won't start, and the payments won't stop.

Two men were watching a fight between two dogs. "Why is the small dog scaring off the big dog?" one man asked.
   The other man smiled. "It is not the size of the dog in a fight that matters," he said. "What matters is the size of the fight in a dog."

In the good old days, people quit spending when they ran out of money.

There are no idle rumors. Rumors are always busy.

Do you feel dog-tired at night? It may be because you growled all day.

The horn that's tooting loudest is the one that's in the fog.

It is good to be on the right track. But remember, if you just sit there, you may get hit by a train.

A sign on the window of a bus station: If you have nothing to do, don't do it around here.

There is nothing much wrong with sleep . . . just don't sleep too much.

Those who tell white lies soon become color-blind.

A great many so-called "open minds" should be closed for repairs.

To love the whole world for me is no chore. My tough problem is the neighbor next door.

Learn from the mistakes of others. You won't live long enough to make them all yourself!

It is a shame if you have more dollars than sense.

It is hard to be poor . . . but not as hard as being in debt.

That money talks is plain to see;
It always says good-bye to me!

When it comes to giving, some people stop at nothing!

Don't just grow old, grow up!

They can't call you an old dog if you are still learning new tricks.

The best thing about growing old is that it takes a long time!

It is OK to hold up your head. Just don't turn up your nose.

If revenge is sweet, why does it leave such a bitter taste?

Beware of a half-truth. You may have gotten the wrong half.

Smiles never go up in price or down in value.

Smiles add a lot to your face value.

After all is said and done, there is much more said than done.

A lady was flying in an airplane. She looked out the window and saw one of the engines on fire. Then she saw a second engine burning, too. "We're on fire!" she shouted. "We're on fire! We're going to crash!"

   Soon everyone on the plane was in a panic. Then the pilot came out. He was wearing a parachute on his back. "Please be calm, don't worry," he told them all. "I'm going for help."

Two boys went to an art show. They came to one wild abstract painting. They looked it over for a minute. Then one said, "We'd better get out of here fast."

   "Why?" asked the other.

   "If they find us here," the first boy answered, "they'll blame us for doing this."

Did you hear about the bald man who kept reading "hair-raising" stories?

Who is the smallest man in the Bible?
The soldier who "slept on his watch."

Who was the best actor in the Bible? Samson. He "brought down the house."

My body is all messed up. My nose runs and my feet smell.

Harry was standing and cheering at a crowded football game. "Sit down in front!" said a voice behind him.
    "I can't," said Harry. "I don't bend that way."

Joe: I could have been a pro bowler.
Moe: Why aren't you?
Joe: It wasn't up my alley.

Joe: Did you hear about the preachers who formed a bowling team?
Moe: No, what is the team called?
Joe: The Holy Rollers.

Joe: I've mixed up a great new morning drink.
Moe: Great! What's in it?
Joe: Yeast and shoe polish.
Moe: What does it do?
Joe: It makes you rise and shine.

A preacher was talking about how bad it is to drink. To prove his point, he brought out two glasses. One was filled with water. The other was filled with whiskey. Then he dropped a live worm in each glass.

In the glass of water, the worm swam around in a lively way. In the glass of whiskey, the worm curled up and died.

"Now, my friends," the preacher said. "What does this prove?"

One old wise guy in the back pew spoke up. "If you drink whiskey, you won't have worms."

A bronze sign hung on the wall of the church. A boy looked at it for a long time. Then he asked the pastor, "What are all those names up there?"

"Son," the pastor said slowly, "those are the names of people from this church. All of those brave people died in the service."

"Wow!" said the boy. "Was it the morning service or the evening service?"

Joe: We just had a great church service. You should have been there.
Moe: What did the pastor preach about?
Joe: Gossip. And you know what hymn we sang after the sermon?
Moe: No, what?
Joe: "I Love to Tell the Story"

A father said he would buy a puppy for his son. They went to the pet shop to look for one.
"Which one do you want, Son?" asked the father.
The boy pointed to a little dog in the corner. The puppy was wagging its tail with delight. "I want that one," the boy said. "The one with the happy ending."

Once two hunters got lost in the woods. "We must be calm," said the first.
The second hunter nodded. "I have an idea," he said. "I read about this once. If you get lost, you should shoot three times into the air. Then someone will come and save you."
So they did this, but nothing happened. They

did it again. Still no help came. They did it a few more times. Still, nothing.

The first hunter was upset. "What are we going to do now?" he asked.

"I don't know," said the other hunter. "We're almost out of arrows."

The leader of a small country was upset. There were new postage stamps with his picture, but no one was using them. He stormed into a post office and asked why.

"The stamps aren't sticking, sir," said a nervous clerk.

The leader took a stamp, licked it, and stuck it on an envelope. "Look!" he said. "It sticks just fine."

The clerk thought for a moment. "Yes, sir," he said at last. "But the truth is, people are spitting on the wrong side."

Joe: Did you hear about the rope joke?
Moe: No.
Joe: Skip it.

One guy had an awful dream. He dreamed he was forced to eat a giant marshmallow. When he woke up, his pillow was missing.

Joe: So where did you meet your wife?
Moe: At the travel agency. She was planning to go on a trip—
Joe: And you were the last resort!

Joe: I'm on a new diet.
Moe: Really? What's it like?
Joe: It's great. All day I eat coconuts and bananas.
Moe: Have you lost any weight?
Joe: Not yet. But you should see me climb trees!

Moe: I went to see my friend, the doctor. My right foot was hurting.
Joe: What did he say it was?
Moe: Old age. Isn't that crazy?
Joe: Why?
Moe: Well, my left foot is just as old. Why doesn't that hurt?

Joe: My doctor is worse. At my last operation, he left a sponge inside me.
Moe: That's awful! Do you have a lot of pain?
Joe: No, but I'm thirsty all the time.

Randy and Dan had not seen each other for a while. They bumped into each other at a football game.

After some small talk, Randy asked, "And how is your wife?"

"My wife has gone to heaven," Dan answered.

"Oh," Randy said, "I'm so sorry." But that didn't seem quite right. After all, heaven is a good place. So he said, "I guess I mean I'm glad." But that wasn't quite right either. So he changed it again. "I mean, I'm so surprised!"

Harry was seated on a train behind two young people. He heard the young man saying sweet things to his girlfriend. "Darling," the young man said, "when I gaze into your eyes, time ceases."

It sounded very sweet. So Harry thought he'd try the same thing on his girlfriend. That night he went out with her. At one special moment, he put his arm around her. Then he whispered, "Darling, when I see your face . . . " He tried to think of what the young man had said. "Darling, your face . . . " He couldn't remember it. He thought some more. At last it came to him. "Darling, your face could stop a clock!"

Joe and Moe were walking down the street.
Joe: Hey, Moe, did you see that? That girl smiled at me!

Moe: Doesn't surprise me. The first time I saw you, I laughed out loud.

I never forget a face. But in your case, maybe I will.

A young man was about to give a speech. He was scared. As he began to speak, his voice shook. "Folks," he said. "I'm sure this speech is going to be very good. My knees are already clapping for me."

Mother: Now, Bobby, you must eat your spinach. It will put color in your cheeks.
Bobby: Yes, but who wants green cheeks?

Karen: I caught my boyfriend flirting.
Mary: Yes, that's how I caught mine, too.

Joe: I hear your wife is quite a gossip.
Moe: Yes, she has a great sense of rumor.

Joe: Have I ever told you about my grandchildren?
Moe: No, and I'd like to thank you for that.

Joe: You know my secret of good health? I eat raw onions.
Moe: But how do you keep it a secret?

Each day of his life, Uncle Bob thought something was wrong with him. He always said he was sick. But whenever he went to a doctor, the doctor said he was fine. He drove his parents crazy. Then he drove his wife crazy. Then he drove his children crazy. Uncle Bob lived to be ninety-five. And do you know what it says on his tombstone? "I told you so."

Joe: Say, Moe, did you ever study history?
Moe: No. I think it's better to let bygones be bygones.

Two old friends met at Niagara Falls. "What are you doing here?" one asked.

The other replied, "Well, I just got married. I'm on my honeymoon."

"That's great!" said the first. "And where's your bride?"

"Oh, I didn't bring her. She's been here before."

JUST FOR FUN

John was watching football games on TV all day. He fell asleep in the easy chair.

The next morning, his wife had to wake him up for work. "Get up, dear," she said. "It's twenty to seven."

He woke up right away. "Who's winning?" he asked.

Wife: Darling, the man next door kisses his wife each time he sees her. Why don't you do that?
Husband: I'd like to. But I don't think I know her well enough.

Joe: Why do your parents call you "Haystack"?
Moe: It comes from when I was a kid. I was always doing something wrong. They kept saying to me, "That's the last straw!"

Joe: I always do my hardest work before breakfast.
Moe: What's that?
Joe: Getting out of bed.

There was a young man from Peru
Who dreamed he was eating a shoe.
He woke up that night

With a very bad fright,
And found that the dream had come true.

Joe: You're a good friend, Moe. There isn't a single thing I wouldn't do for you.
Moe: And there isn't a single thing I wouldn't do for you.
Joe: Maybe that's why we have never done a single thing for each other.

A woman was feeling depressed. So she went to her pastor for help.

"Hmmmm," he said. "Did you wake up grumpy this morning?"

"No, I just let him sleep."

They say that money talks. But these days a dollar doesn't have enough cents to say much.

You know why it's so hard to save money? Our neighbors are always buying something that we can't afford.

A boy came home from Sunday school. He dug into his pockets and pulled out a fistful of coins. He had pennies, dimes, nickels, and quarters.

"Where did you get that money, Son?" his father asked.

"At church," the boy answered. "They had two plates full of it!"

The young woman sang a solo in church. After the service, a kind lady said, "You have a very mellow voice." She felt good about that. But she wasn't sure what the lady meant by *mellow*. So she went home and looked it up. To her dismay, the word was defined as "overripe and almost rotten."

Joe: I feel lousy today.
Moe: I feel even worse than you. My head is splitting.
Joe: I feel like I have a hole in my head.
Moe: Me, too. I feel like I have two holes in my head.
Joe: That's what I can't stand about you, Moe. You are always "holier than thou."

A college student was taking a class for the second time. It came time for final exams, and the teacher handed out the tests. "Sir," the student asked, "isn't this the same test you gave last year?"

"Yes," the teacher said. "But I have changed the answers."

Doctor: And what is your problem?
Patient: I feel like a dog.
Doctor: And how long have you had this problem?
Patient: Since I was a puppy.

Eve: Adam, do you really love me?
Adam: Yes, Eve. There's no one else but you.

He sent his picture to the Lonely Hearts Club. The reply came back: "We're not that lonely."

The teenage girl brought her boyfriend home after their date. But it was getting late. Her father called down from upstairs. "Doesn't that young man know how to say good-night?"

"I'll say he does," the girl answered.

The young man talked on the phone with the girl he loved. "Darling, I would climb any mountain for you. I would swim any sea just to be with you. I would cross the burning desert. I would go through floods and fire to be by your side. Good night, my love. I'll come over Thursday — if it doesn't rain."

Girl: Am I the only girl you have ever kissed?
Boy: Yes, and by far, you're the best-looking.

"Waitress," the man yelled. "This coffee tastes like mud."

"Doesn't surprise me," she answered. "It was ground this morning."

Teacher: David, where do bugs go in the wintertime?
David: Search me.

Dad: This is an awful report card. There is nothing good about it.
Son: Sure there is. At least you know I haven't been cheating.

Joe: So, Moe, where do you live?
Moe: With my brother.
Joe: And where does your brother live?
Moe: He lives with me.
Joe: All right. Where do the two of you live?
Moe: We live with each other.

A teacher was trying to get her students to learn new words. "Repeat a new word eight or ten times," she said. "Then it will be yours for the rest of your life."

In the back row, Sally closed her eyes and spoke softly. "Steve, Steve, Steve . . ."

Did you hear about the guy who bought an AM radio? He thought it only worked in the morning.

Joe: I hope you don't mind me asking. Why do you have TGIF written on your shoes? Does it have something to do with the weekend?
Moe: No, that's for "Toes Go In First."

A man from Texas was on a tour of New York State. At each stop he boasted about how things were bigger and better in Texas.

Then they came to Niagara Falls. The guide proudly said, "I bet you don't have anything like this in Texas."

The Texan looked at the rushing water. "Nope," he said, "I reckon we don't. But we have plumbers who could fix it."

Karen: Whenever I'm down in the dumps, I buy a new dress.
Mary: Oh, I wondered where you got them.

Joe: I have a real problem. I forget things all the time.
Moe: How long have you had this problem?
Joe: What problem?

Mom: What did you learn in Sunday school, Son?
Son: We learned about Jonah and the whale that ate him. And how the whale spat him up on the beach.
Mom: And what is the lesson you learned from the story, dear?
Son: You can't keep a good man down.

CHAPTER 4
Time to Work

The person who is *too big* for a small job is *too small* for a big job.

Why does my barber smile so much? Each year his price goes up. And each year I give him less to work on.

His brother has a Ph.D.
His wife has an M.A.
His daughter has a B.A.
But he's the only one with a J-O-B.

The city paper printed a big story. "Half the people on the city council are crooks!" it said. There was a storm of protest. At last the paper gave in. It printed a new story. "Half the people on the city council are *not* crooks," it said.

Mr. Jones had a toothache. He had to go to the dentist. "How much do you charge for pulling a tooth?" he asked the dentist.
  "Forty dollars," the dentist replied.
  "Forty dollars for only five minutes of work?"

"Well," the dentist said with a smile, "if you want, I can make it take longer."

Joe: My son the doctor just opened up a new practice.
Moe: Great! I have a friend who's a doctor. He has practiced for twenty years.
Joe: With all that practice, he should be starting to get it right.

Harry was looking for a job. He filled out a form about his past jobs. Then he gave it to the man behind the desk.

"And why did you leave your last job?" the man asked.

"Illness," Harry replied.

"What kind of illness?"

"I don't know," said Harry. "They just said they were sick of me."

One day Frank stormed into his boss's office. "Sir," he said, "I've worked here for twenty years. In all that time I have never asked for a raise."

The boss pointed a finger at him. "That's why you've been working here for twenty years."

Karen walked into her boss's office. "I've worked here for nine years," she said. "And I've been doing the work of three people. I want a raise."

"I can't give you a raise," the boss said. "But tell me who those other two people are. I'll fire them."

John looked for a job at a food store. The boss took one look at him and said, "Yes. I'll give you a job. Sweep out the store."

"But I went to college," John said.

"That's all right," said the boss. "I'll show you how."

Joe: You know what I always wanted to become? A trapeze artist in the circus.
Moe: Why didn't you?
Joe: I couldn't get the hang of it.

Being a husband is like any other job. It helps a lot if you like the boss.

There was a sign at the office of the divorce lawyer. It said: You can count on us. We will do the job for you. Or your honey back.

A woman was telling a friend how she had been married four times. First she had married a banker, then an actor, then a preacher. Now she was married to an undertaker. "You know how it is," she said. "One for the money. Two for the show. Three to get ready. And four to go."

Two men worked at a firm that published music. They were looking over newly written songs.
 "Look at this one," said one of the men. "I have never seen such corny words, such a sappy tune. And it repeats the same notes over and over."
 "Let me see that," said the other. "It could be our next hit song."

Three girls were talking about the kind of men they wanted to marry.
 "I want to marry a grocer," one said. "Then I can get my food for nothing."
 "I want to marry a tailor," said the second. "Then I can get my clothes for nothing."
 "I want to marry a preacher," said the third. "Then I can be good for nothing."

An eight-year-old boy stayed a moment after school. He had to talk with his teacher. "I don't mean to scare you," he said. "But my dad says my grades have to get better. If they don't, someone's going to get spanked."

A man thought he was sick. He called his doctor one night. "Doc," he said. "I'm sure I have a fatal liver disease."
"That's crazy," said the doctor. "A person with that disease doesn't feel bad at all."
"That's it!" said the man. "That's just how I feel!"

There was a sign in a shop that rents out canoes. It said: No Tipping Allowed.

Peter: Should a person be punished for something he hasn't done?
Teacher: No. Of course not.
Peter: Good. Because I haven't done my homework.

CHAPTER 5
Good Thinking

A man once moved a mountain. He began by moving away small stones. (Chinese proverb)

I do not think that I should drink. For when I drink, I do not think.

You are never fully dressed until you wear a smile.

Don't complain because you don't have what you want. Instead, be very grateful you don't get what you deserve!

It's nice to be important. But it's more important to be nice.

You may fool all the people some of the time. You can even fool some of the people all of the time. But you can't fool all of the people all of the time. (Abraham Lincoln)

If you go against the grain of God's laws, you'll get splinters!

A true friend is one who knows all about you and still likes you.

He who is thankful for little enjoys much.

Some people think so much about heaven, they are no good on earth.

One who never asks questions either knows it all or knows nothing. (Malcolm S. Forbes)

A bitter world cannot be sweetened by sour people.

The worst lie is to lie to yourself.

A lie is a coward's way of getting out of trouble.

Change one letter in the word *united* and it reads *untied*. That letter is *i*.

If money is all you want, money is all you will get.

It should not be what you have in your pocket that makes you thankful. It should be what you have in your heart.

It is better to add life to your years than to add years to your life.

You will not stumble while on your knees.

There is one thing worse than a quitter. It is the man who is afraid to begin.

A quitter never wins, and a winner never quits.

Be sure you're wrong before you quit.

The will of God will never lead you where the grace of God cannot keep you.

As a man grows wiser, he talks less and says more.

Having to *say something* is not the same as having *something to say.*

If we take the time to *think* more, we will surely *thank* more.

Do unto others as though you were the others.

It is good to be wise, and wise to be good.

There is a difference between worry and concern: Worry frets about a problem. Concern solves the problem.

If a man says, "I slept like a baby," you can bet he doesn't have one.

You know how to be a smart husband? Remember your wife's birthday. And forget how old she is.

A sign at the high school:
Look Out For Schoolchildren —
Especially When They Are Driving Cars.

We don't know much about the speed of light. But we know one thing. It gets here too early in the morning!

Just when you think you can make ends meet, someone moves the ends!

How can you tell a true friend? He thinks you're a good egg even if you're half-cracked.

Two can live as cheaply as one — for half as long.

CHAPTER 6
Looking Up

Do not be afraid when things go against you. A kite rises against the wind, not with it.

Our strength is shown in the things we stand for. Our weakness is shown in the things we fall for.

Don't be a cloud because you failed to become a star.

Go as far as you can see. When you get there, you can see farther.

To rise to the top, you must first get to the bottom of things.

Try not to follow the crowd. Be an engine — not a caboose.

Those who are willing to face the music may someday lead the band.

Like a turtle, we don't get ahead until we stick our neck out.

If life is a grind, use it to sharpen your wits.

Great chances in life come to those who make the most of small ones.

It is always too soon to quit.

People don't plan to fail. They just fail to plan.

The best way to forget your problems is to help someone with theirs.

Everyone can do something to make the world better. He can at least improve himself.

Be like a postage stamp. It sticks to one thing until it gets the job done.

Success is not gained by lying awake at night. Success is gained by staying awake in the day.

There are many roads to success — but they are all uphill.

He is no fool who gives what he cannot keep to gain what he cannot lose. (Jim Elliot)

If your method is "hit or miss," you will usually miss.

Plan your work — then work your plan.

Attempt great things for God. Expect great things from God. (William Carey)

If God is your partner, make your plans big!

To succeed, you should work eight hours and sleep eight hours. But not the *same* eight hours!

Three rules for public speakers:
    1. Stand up if you want to be seen.
    2. Speak up if you want to be heard.
    3. Shut up if you want to be asked to return.

Advice to speakers: The mind cannot absorb more than the seat can endure.

Sunday school teacher: What are you drawing, Billy?
Billy: A picture of God.
Teacher: But no one knows what God looks like.
Billy: They will when I'm done.

CHAPTER 7
Down Home

Isn't it great the way children always brighten up the home? They never turn out the lights!

The goal in marriage is not to think alike. The goal is to think together. (Robert C. Dodds)

Men and women chasing each other: That's what makes the human race. (Mark Beltaire)

There is one thing all parents can give their children. They can give children their time each day.

Bring up a child in the way he should go. And be sure to go that way yourself.

There are too many dads who tie up the dog at night and let their kids run loose.

I'm not saying my wife is not as pretty as she used to be. She is just as pretty — it just takes her a half hour longer.

Two men were talking with each other. One said, "It's awful growing old alone."

"But you're still married," said the other.

"Yes," said the first man. "But my wife says she hasn't had a birthday for ten years."

Joe: Who's the boss in your home?
Moe: Well, my wife bosses the kids. The kids boss the dog and cat. And I . . . well, I say whatever I want to the flowers.

Joe: My wife and I had a fight last night. But later she came crawling to me on her hands and knees.
Moe: What did she say?
Joe: She said, "Joe, come out from under that bed. Fight like a man!"

Husband: I wish you could bake bread like my mother.
Wife: And I wish you could make dough like my father.

The pastor was talking about sin. "Do any of you know a truly perfect person? If you do, stand up and say so."

To the surprise of all, one meek man stood up. The pastor asked him, "Do you really know a perfect person?"

"Well, yes, sir," he said softly. "I do."

"Then tell us who he is," the pastor thundered.

"My wife's first husband."

I loved her then. I love her now. I love her now and then.

Adam and Eve had two great things going for them. Adam didn't have to hear about all the other men Eve could have married. And Eve didn't have to hear about how well his mother cooked.

The young boy had never seen his grandmother. Then she came to visit.

"Are you really my grandmother?" the boy asked.

"Yes," she said. "On your father's side."

He leaned closer to her. "I can tell you right now, you're on the losing side."

Joe: Are you married?
Moe: Yes, my wife is an angel. Are you?
Joe: Yes, but mine is still living.

They married for better or worse. He couldn't do better. And she couldn't do worse.

Joe: You seem to have a happy marriage. You and your wife get along very well. But don't you have times when you don't agree?
Moe: Oh, yes. We have quite a few times like that.
Joe: What is your secret? How do you deal with those times when you don't agree?
Moe: I never tell her about them.

Mother: Son, every time you do something wrong, I get a gray hair.
Son: Well, Mom, you must have been awful when you were young. Just look at Grandma.

Joe: My wife is an angel.
Moe: What do you mean?
Joe: First, she's always up in the air. Second, she harps on one string. And third, she doesn't have an earthly thing to wear.

CHAPTER 8
Time for God

Has life knocked you down to your knees? If so, you are in a perfect place to pray.

We only really believe as much of the Bible as we practice.

Give your life to God. He can do more with it than you can!

Some say, "See and believe." Faith says, "Believe and see."

Feed your faith, and your doubts will starve to death.

Little faith will bring us to heaven. Great faith will bring heaven to us.

There is nothing you can do to make God love you more. There is nothing you can do to make God love you less. God's love never changes or ends. His love is perfect.

If I really love God, some things I will have to hate.

I have a great need for Christ. I have a great Christ for my need! (Charles H. Spurgeon)

The Lord Jesus (who is God) became the Son of Man so that I (a man) might become a child of God!

Why worry when you can pray?

The purpose of prayer is not to get man's will done in heaven. The purpose is to get God's will done on earth. (Warren Wiersbe)

A good prayer:
   "O God, grant me the peace to accept the things I cannot change. Grant me the courage to change the things I can. Grant me the wisdom to know the difference." (Reinhold Niebuhr)

If you find it hard to stand for Jesus, try kneeling first.

Sinning stops praying . . . praying stops sinning.

Do not face the day until you have faced God.

If God does not seem near, guess who moved?

Put God first, and he will be with you to the last.

God is for us — that is good.
God is with us — that is better.
God is in us — that is best.

The secrets of the Lord are for those who live close to him.

Never be afraid to trust an unknown future to a known God.

The pastor was praying in his strong way. He ranted and raved about the sins of the world. He shouted about the need for God's grace. A little boy heard all of this and leaned over to his mother, "You always say the pastor is close to God," he said. "But if he's so close, why does he have to shout?"

Pastor Smith always preached for only twenty-five minutes. For years he had done this.

You could set your clock by it. But one Sunday he went on and on. It was fifty-five minutes before he stopped. Later someone asked him what happened. "I always put a cough drop in my mouth before I preach," he explained. "It always lasts twenty-five minutes. When it's gone, I stop. But today I made a mistake. Instead of a cough drop, I put a button in my mouth."

The preacher spoke about the fires of hell. In strong terms he warned the people about the dangers of sin. Later a woman came up to him. "Pastor," she said, "I never knew what hell was like until you started preaching."

In the middle of a church service, one choir member thought of something. The oven at home was still on. It would burn the roast beef. She was sitting in the choir up front, so she could not leave. But she wrote a note to her husband. During the offering, she slipped the note to an usher, to take to her husband.

But the usher got mixed up. He thought it was a note for the pastor. As the pastor began to speak, he opened the note. It said, "Please go home and turn off the gas."

The young preacher heard many kind comments at the door. One lady said, "You are truly a model preacher." *That was very nice,* he thought, but he wasn't sure what it meant. Later he looked it up. A model is "a small copy of the real thing."

What can a preacher learn from an oil driller? If you don't strike oil in twenty minutes, stop boring.

The guest preacher asked the head elder how long he should preach. "Preach as long as you like," the elder said. "But the rest of us will be leaving at 12:00."

WORD LIST

a 212	anyone 1	been 9	bowler 1	case 2
about 33	anything 1	before 5	bowling 1	cash 1
Abraham 1	are 40	began 4	boy 15	cat 1
absorb 1	aren't 3	begin 1	boyfriend 2	catching 1
abstract 1	argue 1	behave 1	boys 1	caught 2
accept 1	arm 1	behind 3	brave 1	cause 2
actor 2	around 4	being 2	bread 1	ceases 1
Adam 4	arrows 1	believe 4	breakfast 2	cents 1
add 3	art 1	Beltaire 1	bride 1	chair 1
admire 1	artist 1	bench 1	brighten 1	chances 1
admit 1	as 23	bend 1	bring 5	change 4
advice 1	asked 21	best 6	bronze 1	changed 2
afford 1	asking 1	best-looking 1	brother 3	changes 1
afraid 3	asks 1	bet 2	brought 3	charge 1
after 8	asleep 2	better 10	bugs 1	Charles 1
again 3	at 38	between 2	building 1	chasing 1
against 3	ate 1	beware 1	bumped 1	cheaply 1
age 1	attempt 1	Bible 3	burn 1	cheating 1
agency 1	awake 2	big 5	burning 2	cheeks 2
agree 2	away 2	bigger 1	bus 1	cheering 1
ahead 1	awful 6	billion 1	business 2	child 2
air 2	B.A. 1	Billy 3	busy 1	children 4
airplane 1	baby 1	birthday 3	but 47	Chinese 1
Al 1	back 7	bit 1	button 1	choir 2
alike 2	bad 5	bitter 2	buy 3	chore 1
all 43	bake 1	blab 1	buying 1	Christ 3
alley 1	bald 1	blame 2	by 11	church 8
allowed 1	bananas 1	blocks 1	bygones 2	circus 1
almost 2	band 1	boasted 1	caboose 1	city 3
alone 1	banker 1	boat 1	call 2	claim 1
along 1	barber 1	Bob 2	called 3	clapping 1
already 1	barged 1	Bobby 2	calm 2	class 1
always 17	barked 1	body 1	came 12	cleaner 1
am 3	battle 1	boil 1	can 27	clerk 2
an 24	be 42	boring 2	can't 9	climb 2
and 86	beach 1	boss 8	cannot 7	clock 2
angel 2	became 1	boss's 2	canoes 1	close 3
answer 1	because 6	bosses 1	card 1	closed 3
answered 5	become 5	bottle 1	care 3	closer 1
answers 1	bed 3	bottom 2	Carey 1	clothes 1
any 6	beef 1	bought 1	cars 2	cloud 1

69

club 1
coconuts 1
coffee 1
coins 1
college 2
color 1
color-blind 1
come 5
comes 2
comments 2
common 1
complain 1
concern 2
congress 1
cooked 1
copy 1
corner 1
corny 1
cough 2
could 9
couldn't 4
council 2
count 1
country 1
courage 1
course 1
coward's 1
crabs 1
crash 1
crawling 1
crazy 6
credit 1
crooks 2
cross 1
crowd 1
crowded 1
cure 1
curled 1
dad 2
dads 1
Dan 2
dangers 1
darling 6
date 1
daughter 1
David 2
day 8
days 3
deal 1

dear 3
death 1
debt 1
defined 1
delight 1
dentist 4
departed 1
depressed 1
desert 1
deserve 1
desk 1
did 18
didn't 7
died 2
diet 1
difference 2
dimes 1
diner 1
dinner 1
disease 2
dismay 1
divorce 1
do 48
Doc 1
doctor 10
Dodds 1
does 11
doesn't 10
dog 9
dog-tired 1
dogs 1
doing 4
dollar 1
dollars 3
don't 32
done 10
door 3
doubts 1
dough 1
down 8
drawing 1
dream 2
dreamed 2
dress 1
dressed 1
driller 1
drink 5
driving 1
drop 2

dropped 2
drove 3
dug 1
dumping 1
dumps 1
during 1
Dwight 1
each 15
early 1
earth 2
earthly 1
easy 3
eat 4
eating 1
egg 1
eggs 1
eight 4
eight-year-old 1
either 2
elder 2
Elliot 1
else 1
ending 1
ends 3
endure 1
engine 3
engines 1
enjoys 1
enough 3
envelope 1
especially 1
Eve 5
even 3
evening 1
ever 3
every 1
everyone 2
exams 1
expect 1
explained 1
eyes 2
face 7
faced 1
fail 2
failed 1
faith 4
fall 1
falls 2
far 2

farther 1
fast 1
fatal 1
father 8
father's 1
fatigue 1
feed 1
feel 8
feeling 1
feet 1
fell 1
felt 1
few 2
fifty-five 1
fight 7
filled 3
final 1
find 3
fine 2
finger 1
fire 5
fires 1
firm 1
first 15
fistful 1
fit 1
five 1
fix 1
flirting 1
floods 1
flowers 1
flying 1
fog 1
folks 1
follow 1
food 3
fool 4
foot 2
football 3
for 65
Forbes 1
forced 1
forget 4
form 1
formed 1
found 1
four 4
Frank 1
frets 1

friend 8
friends 2
fright 1
from 11
front 2
full 1
fully 1
funny 2
future 1
gain 1
gained 2
game 2
games 1
gas 1
gave 3
gaze 1
get 28
gets 4
getting 3
giant 1
girl 8
girlfriend 2
girls 1
give 8
given 1
gives 1
giving 1
glad 2
glass 3
glasses 1
go 15
goal 2
God 22
God's 4
goes 1
going 8
gone 3
good 22
good-bye 1
good-night 1
gossip 2
got 6
gotten 1
grace 2
grades 1
grain 1
grandchildren 1
grandma 1
grandmother 2

WORD LIST

grant 3	hear 8	I've 4	later 4	losing 1
grateful 1	heard 4	idea 1	laugh 1	lost 3
gray 1	heart 1	idle 1	laughed 1	lot 6
great 16	hearts 1	if 34	laws 1	lots 1
green 1	hearty 1	illness 3	lawyer 1	loud 1
grind 1	heaven 6	important 2	lead 2	loudest 1
grocer 1	hell 2	impress 1	leader 2	lousy 1
grouchy 1	help 4	improve 1	leaned 2	love 12
ground 1	helping 1	in 71	learn 4	loved 2
grounds 1	helps 1	inside 1	learned 2	lying 1
grow 2	her 21	instead 2	learning 1	M.A. 1
growing 2	here 9	into 10	least 2	made 1
growled 1	hey 1	is 93	leave 3	make 12
grows 1	high 1	isn't 6	leaving 1	makes 3
grumpy 1	him 17	it 100	left 4	Malcolm 1
guess 2	himself 1	it's 11	lend 1	man 37
guest 1	his 41	its 1	less 4	man's 1
guide 1	history 1	j-o-b 1	lesson 1	mankind 1
guy 3	hit 3	Jesus 4	let 4	many 4
habits 1	hold 1	Jim 1	letter 2	mark 1
had 23	hole 1	job 10	letting 1	marriage 2
hair 2	holes 1	jobs 2	licked 1	married 8
hair-raising 1	holier 1	Joe 56	lie 3	marry 5
half 6	holy 1	John 3	lies 1	marshmallow 1
half-cracked 1	home 8	joke 1	life 8	Mary 2
handed 1	homework 1	Jonah 1	life's 1	matters 2
hands 1	honey 1	Jones 1	light 1	may 6
hang 1	honeymoon 1	joy 2	lights 1	maybe 2
happen 1	hope 1	just 20	like 24	me 24
happened 2	horn 1	Karen 3	likes 1	mean 4
happy 2	hot 1	keep 7	Lincoln 1	meant 2
hard 5	hour 3	kept 2	listens 1	meek 1
hardest 2	hours 3	kid 1	little 6	meet 2
hardware 1	house 2	kids 3	live 10	mellow 2
harps 1	how 21	kind 5	lived 1	member 1
Harry 7	human 1	kissed 1	lively 1	men 8
has 9	hundredth 1	kisses 1	liver 1	men's 1
hasn't 2	hung 1	kite 1	lives 2	messed 1
hate 1	hunter 3	kneeling 1	living 1	met 1
have 53	hunters 1	knees 4	lonely 2	method 1
haven't 2	hurry 1	knew 1	long 10	middle 1
having 2	hurt 1	knocked 1	longer 3	might 1
haystack 1	hurting 1	know 21	look 6	mind 3
he 112	husband 7	known 1	looked 7	minds 3
he'd 1	hymn 1	knows 6	looking 2	mine 2
he'll 1	I 148	lady 4	looks 1	minute 1
he's 2	I'd 3	last 12	loose 1	minutes 5
head 5	I'll 6	lasts 1	Lord 5	miss 2
health 1	I'm 14	late 1	lose 1	missing 1

71

MAKE MY DAY

mistake 4	nose 2	pastor 13	preachers 1	repeats 1
mistakes 1	not 27	patient 2	preaching 1	replied 4
mixed 2	note 4	pay 1	pretty 2	reply 1
model 2	notes 1	payments 2	price 2	report 1
Moe 45	nothing 14	pays 1	printed 2	resort 1
mom 3	now 8	peace 1	pro 1	rest 2
moment 3	of 84	pennies 1	problem 11	return 1
money 10	off 3	people 31	problems 2	returned 1
Moody 1	offering 1	percent 1	protest 1	revenge 1
more 15	office 5	perfect 4	proudly 1	rid 1
morning 7	often 2	person 4	prove 2	right 11
most 2	oh 4	person's 1	proverb 1	rise 2
mother 6	oil 2	Peru 1	public 1	rises 1
mountain 2	OK 1	pesters 1	published 1	roads 1
mouth 3	old 13	pet 1	pulled 1	roast 1
moved 2	oldest 1	Peter 2	pulling 1	Robert 1
moves 1	on 37	pew 1	punished 1	rock 1
moving 1	once 4	Ph.D. 1	puppy 3	rollers 1
Mr. 1	one 51	phone 1	purpose 2	rope 1
much 13	ones 3	picture 3	put 5	rotten 1
mud 1	onions 1	piece 1	quarters 1	roughly 1
music 2	only 8	pillow 1	questions 1	row 1
must 4	open 1	pilot 1	quiet 2	rows 1
my 44	opened 3	place 3	quit 3	rubbish 1
myself 2	operation 1	plain 1	quite 4	rules 1
names 2	or 9	plan 4	quits 1	rumor 1
near 1	ordered 1	plane 1	quitter 2	rumors 2
neck 2	other 22	planning 1	race 1	run 1
need 6	others 5	plans 1	radio 1	runs 1
neighbor 1	our 5	plates 1	rain 1	rushed 1
neighbors 1	out 21	playing 1	raise 3	rushing 1
nervous 1	oven 1	please 2	ran 1	said 73
never 20	over 6	plumbers 1	Randy 3	Sally 1
new 10	overripe 1	pocket 1	ranted 1	same 6
newly 1	own 1	pockets 1	rare 1	Samson 1
next 4	owns 1	point 1	raved 1	sang 2
Niagara 2	pain 1	pointed 2	raw 1	sappy 1
nice 3	painted 1	polish 1	read 1	save 2
nickels 1	painting 1	poor 1	reading 1	saw 3
Niebuhr 1	panic 1	post 1	reads 1	say 15
night 8	paper 2	postage 2	ready 1	saying 3
nine 1	parachute 1	practice 3	real 2	says 8
ninety 1	parents 3	practiced 1	really 6	scare 1
ninety-five 1	park 1	pray 2	reckon 1	scared 1
no 22	part 1	prayer 2	Reinhold 1	scaring 1
nodded 1	parted 1	praying 3	remember 3	school 5
none 2	partner 1	preach 4	rents 1	schoolchildren 1
nope 1	party 1	preached 1	repairs 1	scramble 1
normal 1	past 1	preacher 9	repeat 1	scrambled 1

72

WORD LIST

sea 1	sit 2	splitting 1	succeed 1	them 9
seafood 1	sitting 1	spoke 3	success 3	then 23
search 1	size 2	sponge 1	such 3	there 25
seat 1	skip 1	Spurgeon 1	Sue 2	there's 1
seated 1	sky 1	stamp 2	sunday 4	these 2
second 5	sleep 4	stamps 2	sunny 1	they 42
secret 4	slept 2	stand 6	sure 9	they'll 1
secrets 1	slipped 1	standing 1	surely 1	they're 1
see 11	slowly 1	star 1	surprise 3	thing 11
seem 3	small 8	stars 1	surprised 1	things 16
seemed 1	smallest 1	start 1	swam 1	think 11
seen 4	smart 1	started 1	swap 1	thinking 1
sees 1	smell 1	starting 1	sweep 1	thinks 2
sense 2	smile 4	starve 1	sweet 3	third 2
sent 1	smiled 2	state 1	sweetened 1	thirsty 1
sermon 1	smiles 2	station 1	swim 1	this 19
serve 2	Smith 1	stayed 2	tail 1	those 9
service 6	snap 1	staying 1	tailor 1	thou 1
set 1	so 24	stays 1	take 4	though 1
seven 1	so-called 1	steam 1	taken 1	thought 9
shame 1	softly 2	Steve 3	takes 2	three 7
sharpen 1	soldier 1	stick 1	taking 1	through 1
she 40	solo 1	sticking 1	talk 2	thundered 1
she's 3	solve 1	sticks 2	talked 4	Thursday 1
sheriff 2	solves 1	stiff 1	talking 5	tie 1
sheriff's 1	some 12	still 7	talks 3	time 21
shhhh 1	someday 1	stones 1	taste 2	times 7
shine 1	someone 6	stood 1	tastes 1	tipping 1
shoe 2	someone's 1	stop 6	taught 1	tired 1
shoes 1	something 11	stopped 2	teacher 8	to 179
shook 1	son 13	stops 2	team 2	today 2
shoot 1	song 1	store 3	teenage 1	toes 1
shop 2	songs 1	stories 1	tell 10	together 1
should 12	soon 4	storm 1	telling 2	told 4
shouldn't 1	sorry 1	stormed 2	ten 2	tombstone 1
shout 1	sounded 1	story 4	terms 1	too 10
shouted 2	sour 1	strange 1	test 1	took 2
show 3	spanked 1	straw 1	tests 1	tooth 1
shown 2	spat 1	street 1	Texan 1	toothache 1
shut 1	speak 4	strength 1	Texas 3	tooting 1
sick 4	speakers 2	stretch 1	T.G.I.F. 1	top 2
side 4	special 1	strike 1	than 11	touch 1
sign 5	speech 2	string 1	thank 2	tough 1
sin 2	speed 1	strong 2	thankful 2	tour 1
since 1	spend 2	stuck 1	that 42	track 1
single 3	spending 1	student 2	that's 15	train 2
sinning 2	spinach 1	students 1	the 321	trapeze 1
sins 1	spitting 1	study 1	their 7	travel 1
sir 5	splinters 1	stumble 1	theirs 1	trees 1

73

MAKE MY DAY

tricks *1*	upstairs *1*	we'd *1*	wild *1*	worm *3*
tried *1*	us *11*	we're *5*	will *25*	worms *1*
trip *1*	use *1*	weakness *1*	William *1*	worry *6*
trouble *4*	used *1*	wear *3*	willing *1*	worse *5*
true *3*	usher *2*	wearing *1*	wind *1*	worst *1*
truly *2*	using *1*	week *1*	window *2*	would *7*
trust *1*	usually *1*	weekend *1*	winner *1*	wouldn't *2*
truth *3*	vacant *2*	weight *1*	winning *1*	wow *1*
try *3*	value *2*	well *13*	wins *1*	written *2*
trying *1*	very *9*	went *10*	winter *1*	wrong *10*
tune *1*	visit *2*	were *12*	wisdom *1*	wrote *1*
turn *3*	voice *3*	whale *2*	wise *4*	year *3*
turtle *1*	wagging *1*	what *42*	wiser *1*	years *8*
TV *1*	waitress *3*	what's *3*	wish *2*	yeast *1*
twenty *7*	wake *2*	whatever *1*	with *34*	yelled *1*
twenty-five *2*	walked *1*	when *18*	without *1*	yelling *1*
two *17*	walking *1*	whenever *3*	wits *1*	yes *14*
uncle *2*	wall *1*	where *9*	woke *3*	yet *1*
under *1*	want *15*	where's *1*	woman *4*	yoke *1*
undertaker *1*	wanted *3*	wherever *1*	women *2*	York *1*
united *1*	wants *2*	which *1*	women's *1*	you *173*
unkind *1*	warned *1*	while *2*	won't *4*	you'll *2*
unknown *1*	Warren *1*	whiskey *3*	wonder *1*	you're *7*
unless *1*	was *58*	whispered *2*	wondered *1*	you've *1*
unparted *1*	wasn't *4*	white *1*	woods *1*	young *12*
untied *1*	watch *1*	who *29*	word *3*	your *46*
until *6*	watching *2*	who's *3*	words *2*	yours *1*
unto *1*	water *4*	whole *2*	work *8*	yourself *4*
up *36*	way *8*	why *21*	worked *4*	
uphill *1*	ways *1*	wife *17*	working *1*	
upset *2*	we *30*	wife's *2*	world *3*	